"Queens"

THE EVOLUTION OF THE BLACK WOMAN

Collis Duhart Marrow

authorHOUSE®

AuthorHouse™
1663 Liberty Drive
Bloomington, IN 47403
www.authorhouse.com
Phone: 1-800-839-8640

First published by AuthorHouse   11/22/2011

ISBN: 978-1-4634-4216-3 (sc)
ISBN: 978-1-4634-4215-6 (hc)
ISBN: 978-1-4634-4214-9 (ebk)

Library of Congress Control Number: 2011913013

Printed in the United States of America

Black Scholar Literature
P.O. Box 22964
Newark, NJ 07101
Contact Information: marrowcollis@yahoo.com
(973) 289-7406

"Queens forward"

The Black woman is the earth, she feeds and nurtures the Black men and children, she is the most valuable resource that the Black man has ever had. She is so gorgeous to the eye, yet so strong and self- determined. She is the driving force behind the man and the child. One day a brother dropped a jewel on me by saying "If you teach a man you only teach one, but if you teach a woman you teach a generation", that made a lot of sense to me. In Africa, during the early civilizations, our ancestors would consider wives as being queens, empresses or even goddesses. We must realize that names have meanings and power, so when we address our women by these titles they will feel empowered to play the role of a wife and a queen. They will even manifest strong characteristics of leadership qualities by dictating to nations and demanding respect in critical situations.

In the past, African American men had strong African American women by their sides; I like to phrase this as "the unseen hand". Throughout my life, I have had the pleasure of being raised by queens starting from my mother to my aunts, and also my grandmothers. The women in my life shaped and molded my character by instilling in me good morals and self-respect. Watching positive women gave me a perception of how I would want my wife to be. For every strong man there is a strong woman ever present. This book is dedicated to all the queens throughout history from the past to present. The likes of Betty Shabazz, Corretta Scott King and Queen Nefertiti, to name a few. These sisters were leaders in their own right; they also had a great influence on some powerful Black men. It was their duty to stand up for freedom, justice, and equality. They were advocates of civil rights as well as human rights.

I would like to enlighten my younger sisters in the world about the sisters before them who made great impacts on society. They did not have low self-esteem and parade around nude to gain the attention of men. I want this generation of queens to understand that they are beautiful in their own right and to remember that beauty is in the eyes of the beholder, which means beauty comes from within. To my sisters, you must keep your head held high as well as your confidence. In the new millennium, women are more independent. They are taking on more of the responsibilities when it comes to finances in a two-parent household. When I study history, I see that the Black woman has endured much adversity during slavery times in America. They had to sit back and witness the Black man being castrated mentally and physically. They had to give up the responsibility of raising their own children, in turn, to raise the slave masters' children, and not to mention the years and years of physical abuse and rape. The only person that was on the black mans' side was the

Black woman. Our sisters were our confidantes, and our only resource, and even so until today. The black woman plays a vital role in the upbringing of our future queens. In today's society, the media promotes the "sex sells" propaganda. I am a Black man and feel that a large proportion of Black women are exploited and taken advantage of for little or no gain. Look at the magazines and the television, as a matter of fact, look at any club scene in any major city. A large percentage of our queens are not wearing their crowns properly. Many of our sisters are misguided by false misconceptions of the fast life. I call it the "Cinderella syndrome". The "Cinderella syndrome" is when a woman believes that Mr. Perfect will come into their lives and sweep them off their feet; they won't have to work and be independent, they think their only responsibility will consist of looking pretty and catering to men's sexual desires. Some women feel there is no need for ambition or self-determination and they desire to wait on a man hand and foot. Our Nubian princesses are descendants of some of the strongest queens ever. Each of you, my sisters, has the same attributes and characteristics as Oprah Winfrey, Madam C.J. Walker or even Harriet Tubman, need I say more. These women were pioneers for black women and our future generations will be able to read about the legacy that they left behind.

I believe that many young women today are only interested in looking beautiful and not elevating their intellect to match their beauty. There's nothing like an intellectual woman; I think a brain is so sexy. A woman who has wisdom is the ultimate gift from the "Most High". I love when I see strong Black sisters with leadership qualities and a sense of direction. In the new millennium, these values are ever present in my sisters today, but some are not being the strong companions they should be.

One huge turn off for me, is a woman who is dependent on every man that comes into her life. Many of the old school values and morals of yesterday do not apply. I don't think a woman is attractive if they live by the slogan "sex sells" meaning, they will put a price on their morals and self respect. This is one of the reasons that Black men call women b**ches, like I said before names have power. I am not justifying this behavior from Black men but men judge women by their outer appearance and the image that they project. When I see my sisters wearing very provocative clothing and leaving little to the imagination, it turns me off because I know a lot of men are looking to take advantage and misguide them. I am not writing this book to pass judgment on my people because at one point in my life I was naive as well. My sisters must realize that the way they carry themselves determines the type of men they will attract. If you want to attract kings, you must act like queens. The Black woman is something magical because she demonstrates insurmountable strength. We as Black men must uplift our queens and be more supportive of their ideas, their ambitions and their feelings. Our queens need us to be more fatherly toward them if ever they need a shoulder to cry on. As kings, we must remember that many of our queens are delicate and we have to be careful when dealing with their emotions. The majority of our queens take on more of the responsibilities when the king is not in the picture, possibly due to serving time in prison, street violence, or abandonment. Regardless of the situation, we leave a huge cross for our sisters to bear. Many of our Nubian princesses fall victim to drug abuse, or spousal abuse as well as depression. Through these strenuous times, they still find the power to assert themselves and to raise the family on their own; this is what they call motherly instincts. I learned through my interludes with the female species that I should have been more patient and understanding rather than doing all of the talking, I should have listened more. To conclude, I would like to let all the queens on the face of this earth know that the Black man loves you and you are appreciated, if it weren't for the woman, we wouldn't have these great nations of the world.

"Dedications"

First of all, I would like to thank the "Most High, The Supreme Being, Allah or God" whatever name you choose to submit to. Next, special thanks goes to my dearly departed uncle, Sean Duhart, my great grandmother, Johnnie Mae Johnson, and my grandmother, Ernestine Whitehead. Now rest in peace to my peers and associates who decided to leave the earth before me: Fuquan Ali, Will out of Tampa, Florida, and John. A special thank you goes to my brothers who are in physical bondage but are psychologically embracing freedom, justice and equality. My brothers Mark Mcintosh, Brenton, Kenneth Jarvis, Solomon Dozier, Robert Torres, Rueben Jones, A.K.A. Flip my best man Darius Williams who was a great friend when I lived in a physical state of purgatory. Much love goes out to my first cousins who are fighting their own devils, Terrance Duhart, Anthony Duhart, Trae Duhart and Keith Duhart. A special thanks to the family members who kept me alive when I was dead to the world while physically incarcerated and continue to be a huge influence in my renaissance. A special thanks to my brother "G" I remember those ice-cold winter mornings waiting at the bus stop just to go labor ready for minimum wage. Your conversations were uplifting and motivational. Struggle builds character and patience brings prosperity. Special thanks go out to my big sisters and brothers. Sandy, thanks for supplying me with shelter when I was living a counter-productive life. My brother, William, for demonstrating silence and how golden it is to have as an attribute. A special thank you to my oldest sister, Charlotte Scruggs, for being the perfect example of a strong, single mother, and one love to my niece Robin and my nephew Robert. I want to send an astronomical thank you to my second mother, Debra Duhart Ball, who taught me that knowledge and wisdom are more precious jewels than silver and gold. I can't began to thank you enough I'll just show you in actions and deeds. A dedication also goes out to my little cousin, Danielle Ball. Despite our different point of views we seem to unite when there is a crisis in the family. A dedication goes to my youngest aunt, Henrietta Duhart, whose 44 years old going on 22 and much love to all of her children Nafis, Nadiyah, Atiya, Kevion and their children who are the future generations of our bloodline. In addition, special thanks go out to my Uncle Arthur who showed me a perfect example of a man. A really big thank you goes out to Aunt Christine Duhart and her youngest children, Seanna and Ervin Jr. A special thank you goes out to the person responsible for my existence Sandra Marrow A.K.A "my wisdom". You watched me evolve into a man and just allowed me to make mistakes because you have faith in the Most High and that he would guide me back to the path of righteousness. You had faith in me when no one else thought that I would overcome insurmountable odds. A special thank you goes to my Grandfather, Arthur Duhart, who is the foundation of the family tree. A thank you goes out to my Grandmother, Leila Duhart, who was my mother, father and friend. You were a very stable figure in my life when my biological parents were both fighting the disease of addiction. I dedicate this book to my nephew, Torrey "T-Head" Rogers, and my niece, Victoria Rogers, her husband and their family. Last, but not least, thank you Alfonso Duhart for creating me and much love goes out to his offsprings Khalif, Meisha, Little Al and Gary.

"Ms. Shakur"

Born in New York, NY in 1947, Assata Shakur was an advocate of Black revolution in America. Later she was convicted of murdering two police officers on the New Jersey Turnpike. Born Joanne Deborah Byron in Queens, NY, Assata spent her early years living alternately with her mother-in-law in New York and her grandparents in Wilmington, North Carolina. She ran the streets as a teenager and was eventually taken in by her aunt, Evelyn Williams, a lawyer, who later represented her in court.

Assata earned her General Education Diploma and attended college at Manhattan Community College then at the City College of New York. She became active in student politics, protests and sit-ins. She was briefly married then changed her name to one that reflected her African heritage to Assata, which means "she who struggles" Olugbala "love for the people" Shakur "the thankful".

Around the year 1970, while living in Oakland California, she met a member of the Black Panther Party. Upon her return to New York, Shakur became a leading member of the Harlem branch. There she worked at a breakfast club for school children. Later that year, she joined the (BLA) Black Liberation Army and was accused of robbing several banks, kidnapped enemies, and attempted to murder several police officers in different cities. Shakur was charged with multiple crimes like bank robbery, the murder of a drug dealer and the attempted murder of a police officer. The "Counter Intelligence" program of the Federal Bureau of Investigation investigated her.

On May 2, 1973, Shakur was pulled-over for a minor traffic stop by state troopers while driving with two other activists on the New Jersey Turnpike. A shoot-out occurred leaving an officer and one activist dead. Assata was severely injured. She was treated for her wounds but the medical attention she received was substandard. She endured long terms of solitary confinement and she claimed she was beaten.

Shakur beat one robbery case and a kidnapping case while other charges were dropped due to lack of evidence. During this time, she also gave birth to a daughter who she named Kakuya who was conceived with a co-defendant. In March 1977, she was found guilty of murder and assault and sentenced to life plus 26 to 33 years in prison. Many Black activists viewed her as a political prisoner. On Nov 2, 1979, three visitors to the correctional facility for women in Clinton, New Jersey, pulled guns on guards and forced them to release Shakur. The group fled and she was not heard from again until 1984 when she was granted political asylum in Cuba. In 1987, she published her autobiography *Assata.*

"Ms. Chisolm"

Shirley Chisolm is widely considered to be one of the foremost female orators in the United States. Her character is described as "unbought and unbossed". Chisolm became a politician who refused to allow fellow politicians, including the male-dominated "Congressional Black Caucus", to deter her from her goals. In 1969, her first statement before the House of Representatives reflected her commitment to prioritizing the needs of the disadvantaged. While Chisolm advocated for Black Civil Rights, she regularly took up issues that concerned other people of color such as Spanish immigrants and Native Americans. She also delivered speeches on the economic and political rights of women. She also fearlessly criticized the Nixon administration during the Vietnam War.

Shirley Chisolm was the oldest of four girls; her parents migrated from the West Indies. The Chisolm home was paradise. She received an excellent education in the Barbados Britain school system. She returned to Brooklyn to enroll in Brooklyn College where she majored in Sociology and joined the debating society. She also volunteered in the "National Urban League" as well as the NAACP, where she debated minority rights. After graduating in 1949, she earned her Master's degree in child education from Columbia University. In 1953, as a key member of the Seventeenth Assembly District Democratic Club, she waged a successful political campaign and was elected as a Black lawyer to the Municipal Court. Her career took off in 1964 and she won by a landslide for the New York State Assembly. She authored legislation that instituted (SEEK) which stood for search, education, elevation, and knowledge. This program provided college funds for youths with disadvantages. In 1968, Chisolm won a seat in the United States House of Representatives. In 1972, she became the first African-American woman to run a campaign for the presidency running as a candidate for the people. She said in her autobiography, *The Good Fight,* that she wanted others to feel themselves as capable of running for a high political office as any wealthy, white man.

"Unison"

The bond between a man and a woman is a sacred and righteous act; it is important to the civilizations of the world. It is a great feeling of accomplishment when you become one with your mate as it elevates an individual mentally which will be manifested physically through your actions. A good relationship is when both parties are on one accord. You have to learn that a positive person will attract other positive people as well as a negative person will attract another negative person.

Many individuals in relationships endure trial and wonder if they will be able to cope with their partner's counter-productive behavior. You must remember, my sisters, that when deciding upon a mate you must assess their characteristics and positive attributes. Only then, you will see if you and your mate are alike or unalike. Do you both have similar aspirations, ambitions, morals and spiritual beliefs? These are just a few questions you should ask yourself when examining your relationship. You cannot plan a future with someone who does not have any purpose or goals. Foresight is a very important attribute that determines your success in life and without it you may not succeed.

Next, you must be conscious of the fact that communication is also valuable in any relationship, whether it is a bond between mother and daughter, husband and wife or a businessman and client. You must be patient with your partner and learn the most effective way to communicate with them. You have to respect their opinions, as well as their feelings. My sisters, you and your significant others are teammates just as players on a football team are teammates. Everyone has a specific role he or she plays on the team. In order for the team to be victorious, each person must be in unison with the other person.

Misery loves company, and envious people may become jealous of the relationship that you have with your king. There are some distressful people in the world who, will not want to see you happy. You have to ignore them and stay focused on the task at hand, and keep moving forward in your life. The only way to counter unrighteousness is with righteousness, evil with good, and hate with love. Maintaining a healthy relationship is constant work and just like anything you want to achieve in life, you must work at it.

The word unison means to move in harmony, which is the greatest sound that you would want to hear in music. In unison, the attribute of reliability comes to the surface of the relationship. Speaking from a king's perspective it is a glorious feeling when a king can rely on his queen at any time or in any situation. Sisters, your being reliable will only help the relationship grow and alleviate any seeds of selfishness that may seep into your mind and annihilate your righteous character.

The Black family is essential to the future civilizations of America. History shows that the Black family has been divided throughout centuries in America. My sisters, the strengthening of relationships starts with each individual being conscious of others' opinions. It is vital to remember that a "house that is divided cannot stand," meaning that the mother and father cannot oppose one another and bring up a child properly.

Commitment is indispensible because it builds trust between you and your mate. It allows your partner to know that you can be accountable in the relationship, which will contribute to the growth process. There is too much negative propaganda on television damaging the credibility of African American men. Sisters, you have been the African American man's only resource throughout history. Now in the post millennium, the African American man and African American woman have separate agendas and goals excluding one another. From a Black man's point of view, I know there are some evil men in the world that only want to use, degrade and harm the African American woman, but it is only out of ignorance. I am not making excuses for Black men, I'm just saying be more patient with your brothers and don't let outside forces determine the way you perceive African American men. If we do not embrace one another and teach one another, how can we evolve?

"Fannie Lou"

Fannie Lou Hamer was born Oct 6, 1917, in Montgomery County, Mississippi and died March 14, 1977. The youngest of 20 children born to share croppers Ella and Jim Townsend, Fannie began picking cotton at the age of six; she left school to become a fulltime worker six years later. Despite her lack of education, Hamer often spoke of reading. Her childhood was spent in poverty where she lived without heat, plumbing or any nutritious food.

In 1944, after many of her siblings moved north, she married a local named Percy Hamer. In the summer of 1962, Hamer went to meetings in Massachusetts organized by the SNCC, which had recently begun organizing in Delta, Mississippi. The SNCC and other Civil Rights groups hoped to register and educate many of the 400,000 Blacks in Mississippi who were denied their Constitutional Right to vote. Following the meeting, Hamer went along with 17 others to vote in Indianola, where they faced a registration test that was designed for Blacks to fail and it succeeded. When she returned home,

Hamer refused to promise her White boss that she would stop trying to vote. He fired her and threw her off the plantation where she worked for 18 years; she told friends "Now I can work for my people". She soon joined the Student Nonviolent Coordinating Committee (SNCC) after she was unfairly jailed and severely beaten in Winona, Mississippi while returning from citizenship classes. Due to the intervention of the F.B.I., the jailers were tried for assaulting Hamer, but an all-white jury found the jailers not guilty.

In 1963, Hamer and others founded the Mississippi Freedom Democratic Party in an attempt to force the states traditionally all white, racist Democratic Party to integrate. When the Mississippi Freedom Democratic Party (MFDP) was rebuffed in its attempt to seat delegates at the 1964 Democratic National Convention, Hamer appeared on television to "question America" about its failure to provide equal justice for all. Hamer continued her involvement in Civil Rights work, speaking out on issues of poverty and economic justice.

From 1969 to 1974, she ran a freedom farm that provided poor Blacks with food and jobs. In 1976, both Howard University and Morehouse College awarded Hamer with honorary degrees. The congressional Black Caucus also honored her shortly before her death.

"Body Image"

A woman's physical beauty is impeccable from her lips to her hips and all in between. I can recall a time that White America would criticize a Black woman for having a huge behind, by saying that she was fat and unattractive. Now when you fast forward to 2010, it seems that women of other cultures are mimicking Black women by altering their looks through surgeries to increase their breast size and even injecting themselves with steroids to give them fuller lips and larger behinds. I guess you can see the truth in this next statement "first shall be last and last shall be first".

On the opposite end of the spectrum, an epidemic has taken over the Black community and it is attacking our sisters. This epidemic is called obesity. Let us not get the message misconstrued; "big is beautiful" but big can be healthy as well. African American women have the highest rate of being overweight. Many are also considered to be obese. Compared to other groups in the United States, 4 out of 5 African American women are obese. As Black women, you must be conscious of your health and this is a matter concerning life and death. There are many health issues pertaining to obesity. A few of them are heart disease, type 2 diabetes, high blood pressure, stroke, breathing problems, arthritis, gall bladder disease, sleep apnea, and some cancers. My sisters, you need to be more conscious of your food intake and be more active, so you can burn more calories. Sitting in front of a television burns lesser calories than walking, aerobics or even yoga. 50% of Black women are obese and there is no excuses for my sisters letting themselves go without any discipline.

I understand that genetics may play a major role in obesity but it is not an excuse, like "I just had a baby and gained all of this weight". You can control your destiny, my sisters; you can achieve anything your mind can fathom. A lack of knowledge about the importance of screening and testing for major health issues contributes to obesity as well. My sisters, how can you treat the problem, when you are unaware of it? I believe that there is a deep seeded phobia in African Americans when it comes to the medical system dating back to our ancestors. In 1932, 399 impoverished African Americans were infected with syphilis as part of a study. For participating in the study, they were given free meals and free burial insurance; however, the men were never told that they had syphilis. They were only told that they had "bad blood". Researchers failed to treat patients appropriately because at this time there was no cure. By 1947, penicillin had become standard treatment for syphilis. The scientists continued the study where they withheld penicillin and information about it from the patients. The victims included numerous men who died from syphilis, wives who contracted the disease and children born with congenital syphilis. My sisters, you must not only believe in home remedies or let superstitions about health stop you from taking care of yourself properly. Remember, big is beautiful, but it can also be healthy.

I have witnessed so many insecure acts from women due to them being uncomfortable with their body weight. They do not trust men and indulge in immoral behavior and promiscuity only because they feel that their partner does not truly love them. I've noticed verbal assault by plus size women towards slim women; this is another example of women being insecure about their weight. By criticizing another sister because she is thinner is ignorant, just as a sister criticizing a woman because she is overweight these attitudes are the results of low self-esteem.

"Bethune Cookman"

Mary Mcleod Bethune was born July 10, 1775 near Maysville, S.C. She died May 18, 1955 in Daytona Beach, Florida. Mary Mcleod Bethune was a Civil Rights leader, educator and government official who founded the "National Council of Negro Women" and Bethune-Cookman College. She was a significant influence in Franklin D. Roosevelt's New Deal government.

In 1885, she enrolled in Trinity Presbyterian Mission School, with aid from her mentor, Emma Jane Wilson.

McLeod-Bethune moved to Scotia Concord, North Carolina. There she learned "Head-Heart-Hand" education, which emphasized not only academics, but religious and vocational training as well. Her dream was to become a missionary in Africa, so she entered the missionary school known as Moody Bible Institute. After years of study, she applied for service but was rejected because Presbyterian policy did not permit African-Americans to serve in Africa.

After this racist episode, McLeod began teaching at Haines Institute in Augusta Georgia in 1896. In the early1900s, Bethune moved to Palatka, Florida where she established two schools. In 1904, she relocated to Daytona, Florida and opened the Daytona Educational and Industrial Institute. In 1929, the school became the co-educational Bethune Cookman-College.

In1943, Bethune's achievement as the schools' founders and president won her the National Association for the Advancement of Colored Peoples prestigious Spingarn Medal in 1935. She also established the National Council of Negro Women in 1935. By the end of her presidency, the (NCNW) had coordinated the activities of many Black women's organizations, presenting a unified voice to the Federal Government to secure greater equity for African Americans in social welfare programs.

In addition, Bethune had significant influence on Franklin D. Roosevelt's "New Deal" government. From 1936 to 1945, Bethune held the formal position of the Federal Council on Negro affairs, known as the Black Cabinet. She also became director of Negro affairs for National Youth Administration, which was a title she held from 1939 to1943. This made her the highest-ranking Black woman in government at the time. As a director, she fought for racial equality in the distribution of funds to young people and she secured state and local government positions for African Americans.

In the early 1940s, the United States House Committee on un-American activities labeled her a communist. This damaged her reputation; still Bethune's support for Civil Rights was unfaltering. She participated in the New Negro Alliances picket lines in 1939 and she joined A. Philip Randolph's March on_Washington movement in 1941. Bethune was honored with awards for her work as a Civil and women's rights leader all throughout her life.

"Sara Walker"

Sara Walker was born Dec 23, 1876 in Delta, Louisiana. She passed away May 25, 1919. She was born to former slaves Owen and Minerva Breedlove; Sarah grew up in poverty on the Burney Plantation in Delta Louisiana working in cotton fields from sunrise to sunset.

Uneducated as a youth, she learned as an adult to read and write. At the age of 14, she married Moses McWilliams who was reportedly killed by a White lynch mob in 1885, which was two years after their daughter Aleila's birth.

Walker took several chances as an entrepreneur in Black women's hair care products. To meet the needs of women who did not have running water, supplies, or equipment, Walker created a hot comb with specially spaced teeth to soften or straighten Black hair. She also created a wonderful hair product that contained sulfur for women who had experienced hair loss through improper care. Business differences ended her marriage to C.J. Walker, a newspaper man whose advertising and mail order knowledge contributed to the business. Walker was the first woman to sell products via mail order and to organize a nationwide membership of door- to- door agents. She established the "Madam C.J. Walker Hair Culturist Union of America" and opened her own beauty school, The Walker College of Hair Culture. Walker and her daughter A'lelia established a chain of beauty parlors throughout the United States, the Caribbean and South America. By 1914, company earnings grossed more than a million dollars.

Walker also made substantial contributions to Black women's education. She also owned a house in Harlem, dubbed the "Dark Tower" and "Villa Lewaro", a neo-Palladian-style 34-room mansion designed by Vetner Woodson Tandy, the first registered Black architect. "Harlem Renaissance" notables frequented Ms. Walker's homes after her death in 1919. Her daughter took over the helm of "Walker Empires", in keeping with mother's wishes. In 1976, Walker's "Villa Lewaro" was listed on National Register of Historic Places.

"Protect your mind"

The mind is very powerful because it dictates your physical actions. It is funny that the most illuminating part of the human body is not physically seen by the naked eye, which brings me to my next point. You are what you think; this means that whatever image you have of yourself will be projected through your actions. Your mind must be fed the proper nutrients to work accordingly meaning something educational, like reading, studying, or watching some enlightening television programs. What you put in your mind can keep you evolving or it can destroy you mentally, spiritually and ultimately physically.

These are the reasons that you must monitor your television intake, Internet time, and who you choose to associate with because your mind can become diluted with poisonous thoughts. Too many of my queens have let their beliefs be molded by the instant gratifications of life. You must protect your mind from the rap video lifestyle or the public assistance trap that your friends persuaded you to indulge in. You cannot allow these negative women to control your thinking by telling you to manipulate a man for financial gain; you will only be throwing your self-respect out the window. These are only a few reasons why you must protect your mind because every situation in life is psychological warfare, my sisters. You have the power to achieve success so when a negative individual provides you with self-destructive information you must edit it out of your memory because it may be cancerous.

The mind is your greatest asset and it is worth more than silver, platinum and gold. The mind creates the thoughts and ideas to acquire these riches, need I say more. Anyone who was successful in life had to tune out all negative information because it is contrast to positive thought. There are individuals who want you to fail and be miserable in life like them; some people refer to them as haters. This is one of the main reasons why you must protect your mind from any ideas that may cause you to stagnant in life. It does not matter who is supplying the bad information; it can be a friend, relative or an associate. When this occurs, you must examine the relationship and see if they agree with your positive thoughts or oppose them. Once you assess the situation, you can choose to keep them or get rid of them; your success depends on it. My sisters, your body is similar to the earth as you also give life. It is made up of 70% water like the earth, and when you have a cut your body heals itself just the same as the earth re-grows and regenerates itself. The mind can resemble your heaven because your thoughts can cause you to create miracles on this earth by reaching astronomical heights of success. On the opposite side of the spectrum, your mind can be a place that takes you to the depths of hell.

Look at all the evil, negativity, and ignorance that surround our environment, this is manifested by a person's thoughts because they have not learned the importance of protecting the mind. When someone does not protect his or her mind, he or she may commit a horrific act and society may label this individual as mentally insane. Before a person reaches this mentally unsound stage, they had to be exposed to some traumatizing acts. There are individuals who have fits of rage and kill their co-workers or family; this is the manifestation of thoughts and ideas that they have allowed to seep into their thinking. Distributers place parental advisory stickers on music CDs or rate movies as PG or rated R in order to notify the parents of the contents and then it is up to their discretion if the child is mature enough to watch the material. My sisters, you must remember that your thinking determines everything in your life, so you must protect your goldmine because people in this world will seek and destroy any righteous, positive and prosperous ideas that you have for yourself. In the society we live in the thinkers run the world and the ignorant bares its burden meaning that knowledge is power, and what you do not know will hurt you. It is so important for you to keep acquiring knowledge, so you will not fall into that lazy, ignorant and selfish state of mind. You must feed the brain with knowledge in the same way a car only runs off fuel. If you put Kool Aid in a car's engine it, will not move, that is the same as putting constant thoughts of negativity into your brain; you will become stagnated and will not progress. You will become tired and worn out if you abuse alcohol and drugs and you will not be too desirable to kings.

The mind has astronomical power. It transformed a young Black girl from Mississippi in poverty to the first Black Billionaire in America, Oprah Winfrey. The mind turned Rosa Parks from a hard working low class woman in the 1960's into someone who would not submit to an unjust law into an iconic Afro-American historian. These queens rose from very strenuous situations and hardship only to become what they envisioned themselves to be. You cannot give up in the game of life, life is a beautiful thing if you go out and embrace it. You cannot have the fear of failure destroy your ambitions. We are living in the post millennium era where there are millions of opportunities to achieve success. You must not squander your time away because your window of opportunity may close before you know it.

"Nefertiti"

Nefertiti was one of the most powerful women in Egypt's history. Nefertiti's origins are uncertain although many believe she was a princess from the Middle East. She was the wife of Pharaoh Akhenaton who reigned from 1353 to 1336 B.C.; he is famous for the religious reform that he and Nefertiti instituted. Scholars believe that Nefertiti was primarily responsible for these reforms. The royal couple established monotheism in Egypt by abandoning the Egyptian pantheon and instituting the worship of the Sun God, Aton, and requiring all Egyptians to do the same. Scholars believe that her devotion may have contributed to her loss of power. The women whom he had six daughters by, and who in Akhenaton's words "The hereditary Princess, great favor, mistress of happiness... Great and beloved wife of the king... Nefertiti. She disappeared from the history books in the 12th year of his reign.

"Evers"

Myrlie- Evers-Williams was raised by her grandmother, McCain Beasley. She married Civil Rights activist Medgar Evers in 1951 and together they worked for the NAACP to end discrimination and segregation in Mississippi. Medgar Evers was assassinated in 1963 by White supremacist Byron de La Beckwith. After her husband's death, Evers-Williams moved her family to California where she continued to work for the NAACP by speaking publicly about her struggles for Black equality. In 1987, she became the first Black woman to serve as Commissioner on the Los Angeles Board of Public Works. She was elected chairperson of the NAACP in 1994 with William Peters she co-authored *For us the Living* (1967).

"The Victim or Victor"

In the race of life, you can be the victor or the victim. Each word has a definition that is the total opposite of the other one. The word victim means one that is injured, destroyed or sacrificed under any various conditions. A victor is one who conquers, and one that defeats his or her opponent. My sisters, there are only two types of people in this world, a victor and a victim and I am tired of my sisters choosing the latter. A victim is an individual who allows outside forces to determine the outcome of his or her life. A victim has multiple excuses and all the answers to the questions regarding their living situations. Here's an example, just because you receive government assistance does not mean that you cannot go to work or strive for a higher education. Having physical beauty does not mean that a man will take care of you forever.

My sisters, you cannot walk around with the "poor me" syndrome like the whole world owes you something; you cannot blame your mother, father or lack of income for your current unproductive situations. This is a sign of being a victim. The characteristics of a victim are when you see him or her being very bitter and displaying negative behavior or show contentment for a self-destructive lifestyle. I have come across too many potential queens who have settled for less and have become content with ignorance and poverty. Life is much greater than what our local community has to offer. You must use every situation and obstacle as a learning experience and a stepping stone toward the path of greatness. Who really wants to be a victim? When you see a victim of a crime they display attributes of vulnerability, fear and denial.

Now when you see a victorious individual what characteristics do they emulate? Some of the most common are pride, happiness, motivation, confidence and self-assurance. The victor has overcome astronomical odds to achieve his or her goals. The victor had the strength to endure hardship, poverty and racism to reach her goals. The victor never lets her surroundings dictate her actions or sway her away from her path. To be a victor you must demonstrate a mass amount of patience my sisters. Even though you may be a single mother living in an urban area, this does not give you a reason to be lazy. To be victorious is not an easy task in life. Look at the percentage of the people that rise from the ghettoes to reach impeccable heights in life. Even though it may be a small percentage, you must read, study and keep being persistent and resilient. For your situation to change your thinking must change first. When you have the same old thinking and commit the same old actions you will only get the same results. Change is good, you must be humble enough to embrace new ideas and have the strength to walk down the path of the unknown. When you acquire knowledge and education you realize how ignorant you were before you acquired the knowledge and this only makes you more equipped to take on any difficulties you may face in the future. Everything comes into existence with a thought first. A thought gives birth to a strategy which grows into a purpose which in turn drives you down the path of success, and at the end you'll be the victor. Everyone loves a winner in America especially if he or she rose from rags to riches. When you are a success your family and friends are more willing to embrace you and the media is always promoting a success with positive propaganda. How does a loser get embraced? No one knows a loser or wants to be affiliated with one; they only receive negative feedback if any at all they lose all respect from family and friends because they took on the role of a victim. When a person comes with excuses why they can't achieve their goals, because of racism, illiteracy or their aren't any jobs hiring these are excuses to give up and become a victim. Too many successful individuals in life have used these impediments to fuel their passion to become successful. Anyone who was successful in life had to overcome some insurmountable odds, and it doesn't matter what line of work your in. You must remember that struggle is ordained from the "most high" and in order to overcome it you demonstrate positive attributes; this is the only way, my sisters.

Kings love strong queens. A queen has certain qualifications and duties that she must uphold because of her title. A queen is mentally fit to run the castle when the king is not present. A queen is equal to the king, so she must be able to lead the people righteously. I have written historical facts about some powerful women in this book because they were all queens and victors who took their destiny into their own hands. Nothing was given to them, so playing the role of the victim was not an option for them at all. My sisters, you can achieve anything your heart desires, but it will be constant work. However, this is the only way to become a victor and not a victim.

"Corretta"

Born April 27, 1927 in Marion, Alabama, Corretta Scott King was the widow of slain Civil Rights leader Martin Luther King Jr. She was long active in the fight for Civil and Human rights. Coretta grew up in rural Alabama where she helped her family pick cotton and tend the farm. Her father hauled lumber for a White sawmill owner which enabled him to purchase his own sawmill. The local White community resented her family's success. Vandals burned the saw mill and their house to the ground.

Shaken by her family's trial she dreamed of moving North so she focused on her education, enrolling in a local private high school, where she pursued her talent in music. In 1945, she won a scholarship to Antioch College in Yellow Springs, Ohio. In 1951, King entered the New England conservatory of music in Boston on a scholarship.

She married Martin Luther King Jr. then a Doctoral student in theology at Boston University, in 1953. Her marriage to King was a pivotal point in her life. They returned to Montgomery,

Alabama where he was a pastor at Dexter Ave. Church. The following years she raised their four children and stood by her husband at the forefront of the Civil Rights Movement. In 1962 after the families move to Atlanta she taught voice lessons at Morris Brown College while staying Loyal to her husband. She joined him in Civil Rights demonstrations throughout the south, led marches, spoke at rallies and organized fund raising events at which she lectured and performed.

After the assassination of her husband in 1968, Corretta continued to lead major demonstrations in support of striking workers and the poor, and organized marches to promote Dr. Kings principles, like the 20th anniversary March on Washington in 1983. In 1969, she founded the Atlanta-based Martin Luther King Jr. center for non-violent social change where she served as the center's president and chief executive officer. She maintained a high profile in the United States and South Africa to protest the Apartheid. In 1986 she prevailed in her campaign to establish a National Holiday honoring Dr. King.

"Hush Hush"

Throughout American history, African American women have faced multiple counts of gender inequality and fall victim to the intersection category. African American women receive very little justice by the judicial system, when it pertains to rape, molestation and sexual harassment cases.

African American women have no affect on the prosecution, conviction, and sentencing of their attacker. Race has a big impact on prosecution when sentencing their attacker, what determines the verdict depends on victim's ethnicity, jurors' ethnicity and the relationship between the victim and the defendant. These injustices against Black woman have been taking place since slavery times how have Black woman endured this rape epidemic.

Before the Civil War, slave masters would sexually assault the African American women. The rape of an African American woman was also a tool used by White Americas for economical gain because of the increased labor force. During slavery times when the slave master controlled the African

American women physically and mentally, he controlled the African American household and instilled an impediment between the African American woman and the African American man.

This barrier still exists in 2010 in the relationship between the African American woman and the African American man. History also plays a great role in the prosecution of rape cases today. An African American woman is less likely to disclose the rape to family or to a crisis center. She is also less likely to report it to the police. A large percentage of rape victims endure some psychological deficiencies, which alters their thinking into believing in rape myths, such as the victims may be responsible for getting themselve's raped. However, when an African American woman does report the rape the prosecutor puts less emphasis on getting justice for the victim. I have asked several women who are in same sex relationships said that by being raped they became self- conscious and began to wear baggy clothes, became insecure with their bodies and turn to the alternative lifestyle of lesbianism. This only creates more separation and turmoil between the African man and the African American woman. I dislike when I hear sisters belittling Black men's feelings as if they are better off without them. This way of thinking only causes division and needs to cease. I sometimes ask myself, "If a Spanish woman feels as if she can do without a Spanish man or a White woman belittling a White man and always criticizing him instead of supporting his beliefs and thoughts" why are we separated from one another. After a woman has been raped by a man this creates a constant hate mentality toward every man she may meet in the future.

Did you know that 17.6% of women in the United States have survived a completed or attempted rape? Of these 21.6% were younger than age 12 when they were first raped and 32.4% were between the ages of 12 and 17. 64% of women who reported being raped, physically assaulted, or stalked since age 18 were victimized by a current or former husband cohabiting partner, boyfriend or date. The National College's women sexual victimization study estimated that between 1 in 4 and 1 in 5 college women experience completed or attempted rape during their college years. Every two minutes someone is sexually assaulted. Fewer than half 48% of all rapes and sexual assaults are reported to the police. Rape victims often experience anxiety, guilt, nervousness, phobias, substance abuse, sleep disturbances, depression, alienation, sexual dysfunction and aggression. They often distrust others and replay the assaults in their mind and they are at increased risk of future victimization. In 2000, nearly 88,000 children in the United States experienced sexual abuse.

footnotes:www.feminist.com

footenote:www.brandeis.edu

"Cleopatra"

Cleopatra was the second daughter of Ptolemy Auletes, king of Egypt. The dynasty's founder had come from the Greek speaking region of Macedonia with Alexander the Great and established a kingdom in Alexandria after Alexander's death in 323 B.C.

Upon her father's death in 51 B.C., Cleopatra became queen at age 18 along with her 15-year-old brother Ptolemy. Ptolemy, encouraged by his advisors, exiled Cleopatra and claimed the throne as his own. Cleopatra assembled an Army from Syria, but could not assert her claim to the throne until Julius Caesar arrived. Cleopatra intended to restore the Ptolemic Empire, which had stretched as far as Syria. Realizing Caesar's importance to her struggle she enlisted his help. The two triumphed in 47 B.C. They executed Ptolemy and restored Cleopatra to joint rule with her young Ptolemy (?)

During the conflict, Caesar and Cleopatra became lovers, either out of love or out of political ambition. When Caesar returned to Rome in 46 B.C. Cleopatra went with him. In

Rome, she gave birth to a son, Caesarion. She was still in Rome when Caesar was assassinated in 44 B.C. Then Cleopatra poisoned her brother, Ptolemy and returned to Egypt with her son where she renamed him Coregant.

Caesars' apparent successor, Mark Antony, met Cleopatra in 41 B.C. The two fell in love and Antony went to Egypt where he treated her as ruler of an independent nation. In the same year she gave birth to twins. Antony began a campaign against the Parthians in present day Iran in 36 B.C. Cleopatra joined him at Antioch, where they married. Antony returned to Alexandria, where he and Cleopatra plotted the conquest of Rome and the creation of a shared empire with their joint offspring as heirs. Receiving false reports of Cleopatra's death Antony killed himself. Eventually, she killed herself by taking poison. When her son Caesarion was killed the Ptolemic Dynasty, which worked so hard to maintain, ended.

"Defeat is Temporary"

This is a very interesting topic because so many individuals who suffer from defeat seem not be able to endure it and ultimately become content with failure. The truth about defeat is that it is only temporary and it does not have to be eternal, and that you can defeat, defeat. Never forget that your mind controls your perception of the world and that any obstacle can be overcome by resilience and perseverance. Too often in life we've faced trial and it seemed as if our predicament wouldn't get any better and we were ready to except failure and quit the solution to our problem presents itself. We did not have enough patience to endure the hardship and we did not understand that defeat is only temporary. That is the beautiful essence of time. It can't rain forever and the sun will eventually shine; that is the law of the universe, no one in life has ever been successful without enduring temporary or multiple setbacks. You cannot get too frustrated when dealing with a temporary defeat because self- destruction may occur and this is why my sisters you must strategize contain your composure and assess the problem thoroughly before making an irrational decision. At these times of struggle, your decision-making skills are very vital because your success is at stake. So many individuals were on the brink of greatness when all of a sudden they quit because the task became too difficult, failure is a part of the process in becoming victorious. You must be strong enough to endure the suffering in order to achieve your goals. Struggle builds character your tolerance level will elevate throughout the ordeal, so the next time you face an impediment you will embrace it with confidence knowing that you will make it through it. A lot of people give up on their dreams because they are not emotionally strong enough to pursue their goals, regardless of how tired and strenuous the work may get. Repetition is equivalent to success, meaning you must work around the clock to critique and prefect your technique and method until it becomes second nature. If you run into any barriers it will not frustrate you, tear you down emotionally, and keep you in a psychological stagnant state of mind. Routine is of very importance in life because it brings structure and order to your everyday lifestyle it produces self-discipline, which is key to your elevation mentally. You will achieve anything you set your sights on. No outside forces can impede your progress or detour you from the path of success, the only person that can stop you, is you. The world is full of people who had potential but ended up homeless and poverty-stricken; they perish before finding their purpose for existing on earth. We are living in the post millennium era where opportunity is abundant and you can attain any dream you have. Success is similar to a marathon and not a 100-yard dash because it doesn't happen overnight. There's a certain amount of time that must be invested in the project before you can reach the pinnacle of the endeavor. You may stumble, trip and fall but a resilient person will endure the bad times and keep striving toward your peak. Education is important to elevation, my sisters; you don't have to depend on public assistance forever because it only keeps you content with mediocracy and create low expectations of yourself pyschologically. You must activate your initiative to reach your potential in life. Laziness is one of the attributes that has dominated alot of my sister's character. Once laziness settles in the mind it brings along his friend defeat, which causes you to mentally die over a period of time. You cannot be successful without initiative and drive my sisters these two attributes must be present in your life in order to excel.

"Mrs. Shabazz"

Betty Hajj Bahiyah Shabazz was an American educator and widow of Black leader Malcolm X who became an international Black cultural icon symbolizing the growing influence of Malcolm's name and nationalist message. Betty was the daughter of Shelman Sandlin and a woman named Sanders. Born Betty Sanders, she grew up as a foster child in Detroit, Michigan. As a youth, she was active in her local African Methodist Episcopal church. She attended Tuskegee for a short period of time but moved to New York to escape southern racism and to study nursing.

During her junior year, she attended the Nation of Islam's Temple NO.7 in Harlem. There she taught a women's health and hygiene class and was noticed by Malcolm X. He proposed by telephone and married her in 1958. They became parents of six daughters Attallah, Qugilah, Illyassah, Gamilah, Malaak, and Malikah. Betty was pregnant with the twins ,Malaak and Malikah, when Malcolm was assassinated in Audubon

Ballroom in New York City on Feb 21, 1965, which was an event that she and her children witnessed.

After Malcolm's death, she continued her education in which she received a Ph.D. in educational administration at the University of Massachusetts in 1975. She taught health and science and became head of public relations at Medgar Evers College in Brooklyn. She exited the Nation of Islam but took the Hajj to Mecca, and considered herself a Sunni Muslim. She believed Malcolm had been murdered by the nation and said so in interviews until a public reconciliation in 1995 with Louis Farrakahn.

"Angela"

Angela Davis was in so many ways born into the heart of the Civil Rights struggle. Born in the middle class section of Birmingham, Alabama, that was known as Dynamite Hill for the many Ku Klux Klan bombings that occurred there. Her mother and grandmother encouraged her to fight in the Civil Rights movement. Davis helped organize interracial study groups, which were broken up by police. From 1961 to 1965, Davis attended Brandeis University in Waltham, Massachusetts and graduated with honors.

She spent her junior year in Paris; her contact with Algerian student provided her with global perspective on the struggle against colonialism and oppression. Her political commitments intensified in 1963 when four little girls were killed at 16th St. Baptist church bombing. She began her Doctoral studies in philosophy at the Tohann Wolfgang Von Goethe University in Frankfurt Germany. She also earned her Master's Degree in Philosophy in 1969 in a year she also completed the requirements for a P.H.D. During the time,

Davis met Kendra Alexander and they both became active members of SNCC and the Black Panther Party.

Davis was hired by the University of California at Los Angeles to teach philosophy. Despite her success, the State Board at the request of Ronald Reagan fired her once her Communist affiliation became known. The courts overturned the dismissal, but the regents refused to renew Davis' contract.

Davis then became an advocate for Black political prisoners and spoke out in defense of inmates such as the Soledad brothers. After the killing of inmate George Jackson by guards at Soledad prison, his younger brother Jonathan attempted to free another Black Panther from Martin County California Courthouse by taking hostages. Four people were killed in the shoot-out that followed. The guns Jackson used belonged to Davis. Even though she was charged with conspiracy, kidnapping, and murder, Davis defied the arrest warrant and went into hiding. She was then placed on the F.B.I'S Most Wanted list. Davis was eventually arrested in a New York motel. Her being imprisoned inspired "Free Angela" rallies around the world. Davis spent 16 months in jail before being released on bail in 1972; she was later acquitted of all charges from the "Free Angela" movement.

Davis and others established the National Alliance Against Racism and Political Repression. She ran for office in 1980 and 1984 as the Communist Party candidate for Vice President. Davis was a professor of the history course of Consciousness at the University of California, she also authored several books including *If they come in the Morning* Angela Davis "Autobiography", "Women, Race, and Class (1983) and "Women, Culture, and Politics".

"Daddy's little Girl"

Whatever happened to Daddy's little girl? I can recall a saying when I was a youth, that said, "girls are made of sugar and spice and everything nice". Our little princesses used to be so innocent and fragile and when they grew up you had an epiphany of them being independent and responsible. Their priorities were in order women like my grandmother had magical attributes and always had her own special way of showing tender love and care. You could sense that she had a loving and sensitive outlook on humanity and wanted to help everyone she came across.

I can recall a saying from an older wise brother who said, "Little girls need their fathers", I couldn't agree with him more. The father is supposed to be the role model for his daughter's future husband. He is supposed to display the great qualities of a man to his daughter. She is supposed to see how her father respects, loves, and nurtures her mother and demand the same attributes in her spouse.

When the father is absent, our princesses began to look up to any male figure their mother brings into their home. When a woman's innocence is stolen and she becomes contaminated by a man this alters her whole perception of men especially Black men. Our princesses become self-conscious and develop a low self-esteem as well as other insecurities when dealing with the opposite sex. Some of our princesses end up being infatuated with a man that verbally and physically abuses them. Their mind has been altered into a state of abnormality in their relationships. Some of our princesses become comfortable in a state of misery and expect anything from the men in their lives. The men can have multiple women and even multiple families and our princesses will accept these situations as normal in relationships. This is when she begins to think that this abnormal behavior is normal. Now when she enters a positive, healthy and mature relationship she will think that these characteristics of her relationship are abnormal. Whatever happened to daddy's little girl? Daddy's little girl is missing the attention that she should have been given from her father, and now is belittling herself by dressing provocatively and losing her dignity for attention from a male figure; Daddy's little girl has become so dependent on welfare and food stamps, that she refuses to use her ambition to become independent and successful. What ever happen to daddy's little girl? Daddy's little girl wants to be on television and nude in magazines; she is exploiting herself for little or no gain because she feels that she will get the proper attention she deserves. What daddy's little girl doesn't realize is she will not only receive negative attention she may even become involved in more toxic relationships due to the image she portrays. Daddy's little girl forgot that she must be a queen and respect herself because future princesses are watching her and will mimic her every move. Daddy's little girl represents wisdom in the science of life. Daddy's little girl must convert her mind back to a state of righteousness because she is a Goddess.

My sisters, you must know that you are in control of your destiny. You are the mother of the Black civilization. You are the glue that keeps the family together. In this new world that is ushering in the Black woman has to be a mother and a father in the building of our Black nation. These dual roles in parenting are forced on Black women by some Black men that are lazy and just plain selfish. My sisters, I know that at times the world seems to be against you; you do not know how you will pay next month's rent, or how you're going to get school clothes for the children. That is when you look within yourself and analyze your desire and activate your will to survive and provide for your offspring. You will become more creative as a provider and will not resort to counter-productive behavior, meaning using your lower self instead of utilizing your higher-self or higher thinking.

Daddy's little girl cannot allow sex and money to dictate her actions. When a woman doesn't have any education and she cannot support herself financially, she may resort to selling her body. This can expose her to mental diseases, as well as physical diseases. She may suffer from depression, self-hatred, and stress she may be exposed to various STDs including HIV. Daddy's little girl must remember to use protection when having intercourse because you do not know what your partner is up to. My sisters, did you know that Black women account for 60% of the AIDS victims in America? My sisters, I am tired of turning on the television and seeing our people on reality shows or talk shows, which are titled "I don't know my children's father, help me". This is so unattractive; it demonstrates irresponsibility, promiscuous behavior and most of all unprotected sex. Our ignorance is put on display for the entire nation to see. We are a laughing stock because we are on television acting ignorant. These are not the ways of kings and queens. My sisters, you are so sensual with an allure that any man would become submissive to.

You must not forget that you are the Black man's backbone and a key instrument of the Black family. You are a queen, so you will have to rule the kingdom whenever the king is not present. I have a belief that in order to see the condition of the man you must look at the woman. I hate to see my sisters degrading themselves; you are the mirror image of the Black man and a reflection of our struggles and adversity that we face. We, as kings, are not living up to our kingly duties and cannot soothe our queens emotionally and psychologically, so in turn we let them down. As Blacks in America, we have the highest divorce rate. The bond and the sense of family are not in our community as it were in our past. The respect and honor for marriage has gone down the drain. The younger generations are putting the cart before the horse meaning we will have a child with the woman and we wouldn't even think twice about marriage. As Black men, we must acknowledge that we are part responsible for the condition of the Black woman. As a father if you are not there for your princess, she will be affected her entire life. As a boyfriend, husband or brother you must protect the queens and princesses by any means necessary because the enemy will attack you through your weakness meaning the woman, the weaker vessel. We must strengthen them when they need support emotionally because we must remember that the woman is the caretaker of the Black race; her role is very vital to our existence, so brothers we need to show more respect and patience with our queens because that plays a major part on the future Black generations.

"A Mother's Love Shouldn't Hurt"

While conversing with a close friend, she began to elaborate about her childhood and how abusive her mother was toward her for no apparent reason. Upon hearing this startling news, I decided to research the topic about mothers being abusive toward their daughters and I was appalled at what I found. A lot of single Afro-American women abuse their younger daughters out of mental frustration, self-hatred, and jealousy. This is self-destructive behavior for the mother regardless of how stressed out the mother may be. The mother is the nurturer and she is supposed to raise her daughter to be a queen and to have a high self-esteem. The mother is supposed to be her daughter's provider, confidant and her spiritual leader in certain aspects of her life.

How can a daughter respect and trust her mother if she is constantly belittled, slandered and physically abused by the person who is suppose to love her unconditionally? This is a form of genocide that contributes to the broken home epidemic in the African American community. There is supposed to be unity, love, and understanding in any household and the bond between mother and daughter should be undeniably strong. The mother is expected to be the perfect example of what her daughter should strive to be instead of searching for a role model elsewhere.

As a mother, you must understand that your offsprings are your future and when they grow up, they will be a mirror image of you. These acts may be the reason that many young women in this millennium end up in prison for killing their mother. The psychological meltdown must have taken place in both of their minds. Throughout this ordeal, I still hold the mother accountable because she is the adult and a child must be taught the way of righteousness.

As a mother, you must be more patient. When interacting with your daughter and as an adult you have to be slow to speak and attentive when listening. The one thing a mother should know is that if you are observant of your child's actions you'll see what is the best solution for the problem. I have a saying that I believe to be true, which is that it is more difficult to repair an adult than it is to build a child. As a queen, you are to raise the princesses in the way of the truth, equality and independency. The abusive behavior that the mother demonstrates may have been hereditary and could have been passed down from the grandmother to the mother. The mother may have been exposed to abuse by her mother' leaving her ignorant to the fact that this is counter-productive behavior. Counseling can be one alternative for the mother and daughter; they may need an unbiased mediator to help them sort out their differences and find a solution to their problems without hurting each other emotionally and physically.

Some daughters feel that their mother is the reason for what happens with their education, career, boyfriends and partners. The daughter may come to believe that her mother is a victim of her bad father and sympathize with her mother. If a daughter supports her mother's criticisms of her father they may feel more closely bonded. If a daughter says, "no, my father is a good man!" then the daughter may be punished for taking her father's side. The saying that misery loves company applies in this situation because some depressed mothers may sabotage their daughter's happiness, while entangled or enmeshed daughters may sabotage their own happiness to avoid being happier than their mothers. Daughters who identify with abusive mothers may consciously seek partners similar to their fathers and later abuse those men in much of the same way as their mothers abused their father's. They may even seek sympathy as victims as they criticize and provoke their male partners. And after some unsatisfactory relationships those women may withdraw into lonely celibacy or depression.

Some mothers may try to relive their youth through their daughters. They may try to immerse themselves into their daughters' lives or try to be their daughters' best friend. They may try to make their own unaccomplished goals. A lot of mothers cannot keep their composure and become physically violent. Did you know that 82% of the general population had their first experience of violence at the hands of women, usually their mother's, yet 3.1 million reports of child abuse are filed against men each year. Most of these charges are false accusations used as leverage in a divorce or custody cases. I do not want to seem biased in this situation when it comes to being raised by women, but I do recall some brutal beatings from female siblings for my bad behavior. Controlling your rage and fury will limit acts of violence for anyone. This is not for women who already have a flourishing bond with their mother or daughter. This is for the women who experience friction or turmoil with their mother or daughter. You should love one another; mothers encourage your daughters in a positive way and daughters encourage your mothers as well. Your communication airways should be open toward each other, and any discrepancies you all have with one another should cease to exist because in the end, mothers you are the creator and daughters you are the creation.

"Ms. Maya"

Maya Angelou was born Marguerite Johnson on April 4, 1928 in St. Louis, Arkansas. She attended public schools in Arkansas and California and later became San Francisco's first female streetcar conductor. She appeared in Porgy & Bess, which toured 22 countries. During the early 1960's, she lived in Egypt, where she was the associate editor of the "Arab Observer" in Cairo. During the mid 1960s, she became assistant administer of the school of music and drama at the University of Ghana. She was the feature editor of the "African Review" in Accra from 1964 to 1966, and at this time, she was the northern coordinator for the "Southern Christian Leadership Conference", at the request of Martin Luther King.

Angelou came back to the United States where worked as a writer-producer for 20th Century Fox television shows such as *Sister, Sister.* She also wrote the screenplay *Georgia,*

Georgia and *All Day Long* and the series premiere of *Brewster's Place*. She co-starred in the motion picture *How to Make an American Quilt* in 1995.

Angelou has taught at several American colleges and universities including The University of California, the University of Kansas, Wichita State and California State. Since the early 1980s, she has been Reynolds professor and writer in residence at Wake Forrest University. She has also been a prolific poet for decades and some of her collections include *Just give me a cool drink of water fore I die* (1976) and *Still I rise* just to name a couple; she also recited at Bill Clinton's inauguration the "Pulse of the morning". Some reviewers praised her poetic style as refreshing and graceful. They also applaud Angelou for addressing social and political issues relevant to African-Americans and challenging the validity of traditional American values and myths. She calls for recognition of the Human failing, which pervades American history and renewed national commitment to unity and social improvement.

I know why a caged bird sings (1970) is about Marguerite Johnson and her brother Bailey growing up in Arkansas. It chronicles Angelou's life up to age sixteen, providing a child's perspective of an adult world. Even though her grandmother instilled pride and confidence in her, her self- image was shattered when she was raped at the age of eight by her mother's boyfriend. She was so devastated that she refused to speak for approximately five years. The novel concludes with Angelou having regained self-esteem and caring for her newborn son, Guy. With this work being of an African American girl coming of age, this literature had insight into social and political tensions of the 1930s. Angelou's autobiographical works have an important place in Afro-American tradition of personal narrative and they continue to garner praise for their honesty and moving sense of dignity.

"Michelle"

Born January 17, 1964 in a one-bedroom apartment on Chicago's Southshore, Michelle Obama's father died in 1990, which was two years before she married Barack. She graduated from Princeton University with Cum Laude Honors in 1985, and earned a law degree from Harvard in 1988. Michelle worked at a downtown Chicago law firm.

In 1989, she was asked to mentor a summer associate from Harvard named Barack Obama. Michelle initially brushed Barack's advances because they worked at the same firm. Love prevailed and they were married on Oct 18, 1992 and their first child was born in 1999. Natasha and Sasha came approximately 2 years later in 2001. Michelle has influenced Barack tremendously by being supportive and understanding the position that Barack was in.

Michelle also mastered obtaining a career, while juggling being a wife and mother. Discipline, patience and being a responsible were just some of the attributes that were displayed and this shows eloquently that her mother and father's relationship was an influence on her. Because of her parent's love and dedication to each other, Michelle and her brother went to college. She quoted that through their struggles and success she admits that the American dream can become a reality. Michelle said what attracted her to Barack was that they share a similar upbringing as well as the same morals and values like you have to work for what you want in life, your word is your bond, and you must treat everyone with respect.

In the 2004 race, Obama had the support of influential Black business leaders some of whom had closer ties to his wife and they had to him. According to *Newsweek* a former boss of Michelle Obama's a powerful Black woman Valerie Jarret chairman of the Chicago Stock Exchange served as finance chairman of Barrack Obama's U.S. Senate Campaign.

"Dorothy Insurmountable Heights"

Dorothy Irene Heights was an American administrator, educator and social activist. She was president of the National Council of Negro women for forty years and she was awarded the presidential Medal of Freedom in 1994 and the congressional gold medal in 2004. Born in Richmond ,Virginia, she moved at an early age with her family to Rakin, Pennsylvania.

She attempted to go to Barnard College in 1929. However upon arrival, she was denied entrance because the school had an unwritten policy of admitting only two Black students per year. She transferred to NYU earning a degree in 1932 and a Masters degree in educational Psychology. Heights started working as a case -worker with New York City Welfare Department. At 25, she began a career as a Civil Rights activist when she joined the YWCA. She was the National President of Delta Sigma Theta Sorority from 1946 to 1957. While in New

York, she developed leadership training programs, interracial education programs and ecumenical education programs.

In 1957, she was named president of the National Council of Negro Women, a position she held until 1997. During the height of the Civil Rights Movement, Height organized "Wednesdays in Mississippi" which bought together Black and White women from the North and South to create a dialogue of understanding. American leaders regularly took her counsel, including the first lady Eleanor Roosevelt. Height also encouraged President Dwight D. Eisenhower to desegregate schools and President Lyndon B. Johnson to appoint African American women to positions in government.

In addition, Height wrote a column entitled "A Woman's Word" for the weekly African American newspaper in 1960. Height served on a number of communities including as a consultant on African affairs to the Secretary of State and the President's Committee on the employment of the handicapped. In 1974, Height was named to the National Council for the protection of human subjects of biomedical and behavioral research, which published the "Belmont Report", a response to the Tuskegee syphilis study and an international ethical touchstone for researchers to this day.

"Oprah"

Oprah Winfrey was born on January 29, 1954. She is an American television host, actress, producer, and philanthropist, best known for her self titled multi award winning talk show, which has become the highest rated program of its kind in history. She has been ranked the richest Afro-American of the 20th century and also one of the greatest Black philanthropists in American history, and was once the world's only Black billionaire. She was considered the most influential woman in the world.

Oprah was born into poverty in rural Mississippi to a single teenage mom and later raised in the city of Milwaukee. She experienced considerable hardship during her childhood, including being raped at 14 and becoming pregnant; her son died in infancy. She was sent to live with her father, who was a barber, in Tennessee.

She landed a job in radio while in high school, and later she began co-anchoring the local news at the age of 19. Her emotional adlib delivery eventually got her transferred to daytime talk show host. After boosting a third rated local Chicago talk show to first place, she launched her own production company and became internationally syndicated, credited with creating a more intimate confessional form of media communication. She is thought to have popularized and revolutionized the tabloid talk show host genre pioneered by Phil Donahue .A Yale study claims her show helped to break taboos which allowed LGBT people to enter mainstream.

By the mid 1990s, she had reinvented her show with focus on literature, self- improvement, and spirituality. Though criticized for unleashing confession culture and promoting controversial self-help fads, she is often praised for overcoming adversity to become benefactors to others. At age 32, Oprah became a millionaire when her show went national. By age 41, she had a net worth of 340 million dollars and had replaced Bill Cosby as the only African on the *Forbes* 400 although Black people are just under 13% of the U.S population. With a net worth of 800 million in 2000 Winfrey was the highest paid TV entertainer in the United States. In 2006, she made 5 times as much as executive Simon Cowell who came in second place. By 2008, her yearly income was 275 million and *Forbes* International Rich list has listed Winfrey as the world's only Black billionaire in 2004, 2005 and 2006 and the first Black woman billionaire in world history. In September 2010, Winfrey was worth over 2.7 billion dollars; she has overtaken former eBay CEO Meg Whitman as the richest woman in America.

"Abandonment"

Many Black women have problems that progress from their childhood into their adulthood due to abandonment issues. A fatherless household will leave our queens with all types of poisonous characteristics and attributes. They may choose the wrong type of spouse as a mate and endure verbal and physical abuse believing that these are acts of love. They may be lost for an eternity asking themselve's, why their father was not present in their life. A woman will even go as far as blaming herself for his absence. A father is very valuable to a woman because he is the first man in her life and he is supposed to nurture her and instill in her an infinite amount of unconditional love. The father is supposed to be the perfect example of a man, responsible, understanding, dependable, trustworthy, etc. With his presence, the woman will be strong-minded and not naive when it comes to deceitful men if the father had an impact in her life. She will have better decision-making skills and will be less susceptible to disrespecting herself and allowing herself to be put in uncompromising situations. She will choose righteousness over falsehood.

My sisters, I realize that the foundation of your upbringing determines your stability and strength in adapting and prospering in life, as well as in the relationships you engage in. As a Black man, I can't help but feel responsible for the way our Black women may act towards the Black man. She may be harboring hostility extending from an absent father or an abusive relationship. As kings, and having knowledge of our queens' past issues, we should be more patient and encouraging in restoring her sense of trust in the Black man. A lot of my sisters have deep dark issues that may be rooted and ingrained in their conscious due to the negative men that they were exposed to or the abandonment by boyfriends and husbands. This may even be the reason a lot of our sisters may feel inadequate, they may not understand that the men that are abandoning them are weak and have childish issues that they need to confront.

You can see the effect of the seed of abandonment evolved through the media and television. Reality shows are depicting my sisters as ignorant, childish and irresponsible and that's why the Black males' roles are so detrimental in the upbringing of our future queens in America. No child wants to be alone and; little girls are to be protected, secure and loved. The man is supposed to honor, respect and provide for his family, not abuse, neglect, and desert them.

Divorce is another mind-altering factor that contributes to a woman's self-destruction of her inner self. When a child grows comfortable with both parents in the home and suddenly they separate for whatever the reason the child suffers the most. Their behavior begins to alter, and they demonstrate negative attitudes or peculiar actions and even signs of rebellion may surface.

There is another epidemic that I'm noticing a new freedom of expression in women and it's called lesbianism. This may also be a result of an absent father figure. Without unconditional love given by the father, a daughter may look for an emotional and sensual connection with the same sex. I understand that we live in America and you have the legal right to indulge in a same sex marriage but through historical events and biblical times it proves that these are acts of uncontrolled lust. Two women cannot pro-create as well as two men cannot. Under any belief of religion, we know that this type of behavior is not condoned. In America throughout history, the Black man's role as the dictator of the home is belittled or not even respected in society because of the single parent epidemic that has deteriorated our sense of unity and the belief in family unity. All of these situations that occur in young woman's life affect her psychologically which, will be manifested through their actions. So to my brothers reading this manuscript be a little more fragile toward our queens' emotions and feelings because they maybe carrying extra baggage. However, do not forget that they are still the mothers of the Black civilizations of the future.

"Self Degradation"

Self-degradation is something that is conscious in a large number of women in America. When I see a woman humiliating herself for any reason, I begin to wonder if she is aware of how she's disgracing herself by mimicking self-destructive behavior. When a woman verbally abuses her children, it reveals a lot about the mothers character and what she may have endured in her childhood, which may have caused the negative reaction. When I see a woman who has been so promiscuous that they may not know who the father of her child is, this is a sign of self-degradation. My sisters, you must realize that you are valuable to the existence of the Black civilization. You mustn't repeat the counterproductive behavior, which you may have been exposed to because it only keeps a negative thought process going from one generation to another.

Self-degradation is a sickness psychologically, because what human being would embarrass, humiliate and disgrace him or herself purposefully. When a woman is acting ignorant in the public's eye and she says that she doesn't care whose watching her and she is not concerned with others' opinions about her, this seems only to be an excuse. As a queen, you are to conduct yourself with self-respect, discipline and patience; these are a few of the characteristics that true kings look for in his queen. Self-degradation is a learned behavior, which means it can be unlearned. My sisters, you must stay conscious of the fact that as a queen our little princesses will imitate you so you are constantly under surveillance by the younger sisters. Self-degradation is cancerous to your self –esteem and it will slowly eat away at your positive ideas and creativeness that may be your true inner being.

There is something more attractive to a man than a woman's body and that is the power of her mind and her personality combined with her sense of purpose and determination topped off by a nurturing spirit. These positive attributes keeps a king happy and content throughout the relationship. I know that some men have abused women's kindness and have destroyed their trust in men, but those were boys who had a physical appearance of a man but his mentality was that of a child.

Self-degradation causes long-term psychological and emotional issues, but these issues can be overcome by utilizing self-respect and projecting confidence while exerting positive energy. Education and knowledge can defeat any form of self-degradation before these seeds can be planted in your mind. Why would a person settle for less and just accept anything negative in life? My sisters, remember you can choose your attitude and the image you wish to portray so focus on the righteousness and not the unrighteousness. When you do this, my sisters, life will be a little easier to cope with while you're facing adversity. You should stop belittling yourself emotionally and feeling sorry for yourself because these are signs of weakness and this world is cruel to anyone who is weak-minded and easily tossed to and fro. When you look at your reflection in the mirror, remind yourself that you are beautiful and can achieve anything that your mind can conceive.

"Ending Words"

The essence of the Black woman is undeniably the reason for Black men's existence. She is the sun to the man's earth, which means she illuminates his world. The Black woman has bore a tremendous weight on her shoulders since the beginning of time. In the motherland, Africa, the woman would raise, mold and give the children structure with the knowledge of responsibility, while the chieftains would dictate to the tribes and organize the Army. During the Egyptian Dynasties, the Black woman with the title of queen would rule a nation of Africans and keep its economic status prosperous. In America, in the urban areas, I grew up with sisters who had kept the children fed, clothed and with a roof over their family's heads. The women would also make time for studying because it was top priority. Times have changed; many Black women have been brainwashed by television and their environment into believing in the "sex sells" media propaganda. My sisters, by falling into this thought process you will lose your morals and self-respect and become a slave to currency. As an independent woman, you shouldn't want anyone to control you and when I say anyone I'm talking about a person with wealth as well. I understand the power and influence of money; it is capable of moving mountains in this capitalistic society we live in; however, no amount of money should make you question your morals and beliefs. My sisters, there are certain things in this universe that are priceless and cannot be compromised for monetary gain like self-respect, honesty, love and wisdom. Sisters, you must realize that your value may decrease in people's eyes when they see a woman who is disrespectful, flirtatious, and promiscuous.

Too many of our past Black female historians would feel that their sacrifices and trials that they endured were done in vain. Do you understand that the future will become the present and the present will become the past so everything you are doing at this moment will become history as well? You must be conscious of time because the impact you make in life now will be what the world remembers you by. You mustn't get too infatuated with your beauty because it is only skin deep and ultimately it will fade away. Time cannot be reasoned with and you can only succumb to it. Time is the only asset worth more than money because once it elapses you can't retrieve it again. You can attain everything you ever lost in life except time. You can't physically relive your days of youth and you can't get back the time you frivolously wasted away. Time can be your friend if you learn its true value. Time heals all wounds whether psychologically or physically. Everything has a certain amount of time to progress and evolve before it withers away and dies. Nothing in its physical form on this earth last forever especially animals or Homo sapiens. The challenge is what you do with this blink of an eye which is called time. Every living organism has stages in which growth is taking place. For example, when you were an adolescent you did certain things that children do like watch television, talk on the phone and hang out at the mall with little responsibility in life. Now as an adult you should have reached a progressive stage in life. If you are committing the same acts you committed as a youth, how will you reach impeccable status which is what the "most high" created all of us for. We can't just squander our time away on instant gratification because you may stay in that stage of life longer than the "Most High" intended.

A smile comes to my face when I see my sisters successful in life despite the barriers and impediments placed in front of them. I love to read the newspaper or watch the television and see strong sisters projected in a positive and intelligent light instead of in a sexually glorified way. This means she is not being judged by her physical beauty but by the content of what's in her mind. It also means that the future generation of kings and queens will be molded the proper and righteous way. The family structure may be back in order God, man, woman, and child. The children will become leaders for their people instead of looking to be crack dealers, thieves and prostitutes. Their positive morals and knowledge of self will be the foundation of the communities in which they will live in. Great achievements can be attained by understanding the importance of our time on earth, because eventually we will cease to exist. I believe that no one wants to leave this earth without acquiring his or her purpose and reason for existing. That's why in the present you should be acquiring knowledge, loving humanity and standing up to the injustices in society like many of our great ancestors did in the past leaving a legacy for our future civilizations to read about and adhere to.

- Minority women constitute only about 13% of the female population (age 15-44) in the United States, but they underwent approximately 36% of the abortions.

- According to the Alan Guttmacher Institute, black women are more than 5 times as likely as white women to have an abortion.

- On average, 1,876 black babies are aborted every day in the United States.

- This incidence of abortion has resulted in a tremendous loss of life. It has been estimated that since 1973 Black women have had about 16 million abortions. Michael Novak had calculated "Since the number of current living Blacks (in the U.S.) is 36 million, the missing 16 million represents an enormous loss, for without abortion, America's Black community would now number 52 million persons. It would be 36 percent larger than it is. Abortion has swept through the Black community like a scythe, cutting down every fourth member."

- A highly significant 1993 Howard University study showed that African American women over age 50 were 4.7 times more likely to get breast cancer if they had had any abortions compared to women who had not had any abortions.

MORE TO CONSIDER:

Fox News Covers Protest In Washington DC

Amos and Andy in ~ Black Responsibility ~ - Pastor Childress Article

Abortion Causing 'Black Genocide,' Activists Say (CNSNews.com)

Center For Disease Control Report On Black Abortions

"Dawning of a King's Dream" by LEARN New Jersey Director Clenard H. Childress

"Black Leadership's Misplaced Priorities" by LEARN New Jersey Director Clenard H. Childress

"Black Leadership Owes Don Imus An Apology" by LEARN New Jersey Director Clenard H. Childress

"The Complete Story on Barack Obama"

"Abortion Industry Decimating Black Community" by Charlene Israel

Cincinnati prepares for NAACP convention The Daily Black Pro-Life Advocates Plan Massive Abortion Protest Outside NAACP Mtg LifeNews article

Barack Obama Best Thing To Happen To End Black Genocide

The Best Thing To happen To End Black Genocide

African American Attitudes toward Domestic Violence and DV Assistance

Vetta Sanders Thompson, Ph.D. & Anita Bazile, Ph.D.

Current data indicate that despite a more than two-decade decline, African American women continue to experience a higher rate of intimate partner homicide compared to women of other races. In addition, African American women's rates of intimate partner violence are higher than every other group's, except American Indian women (U.S. Department of Justice, 2001). Contrary to expectation, African American women are more likely to make reports of intimate violence to the police than women of other racial/ethnic groups (Rennison, 2001). National surveys of prevalence and a growing body of literature on domestic violence among African American women have highlighted the need for data on attitudes toward DV services, perceptions of treatment/intervention needs, and evaluation of DV programs in the African American community. Advocates and practitioners have voiced concern over the lack of research that addresses why African American women are less likely to access victim services (National Violence Against Women Prevention Research Center, 2001).

There are few studies examining the needs of African American women experiencing domestic violence. Studies suggest that African American women do use domestic violence services (Thomas, 2000; Sullivan & Rumptz, 1994; Gondolf, Fisher, McFerron, 1988). Gondolf, et al. (1988) noted that most women, regardless of race or ethnicity, sought the same amount but different kinds of help, such as financial support from social services agencies or family, shelter services, counseling from ministers, friends, or agencies; as well material items from friends, family, or agencies. This early study using Texas shelter data (N=5708) indicated that African American women were more likely to call a minister or the police. Sullivan & Rumptz, (1994) suggest that African American women may seek services at the point that violence becomes life threatening, with African American women reporting more severe abuse in the 6 months prior to entering a shelter than European American women.

African American women benefit from domestic violence services. For instance, Sullivan and Rumptz (1994) indicated that African American women who received advocacy services were more satisfied with their stay and had a higher quality of life at follow-up. These services included assistance with education and acquisition of household items. After services were received, African American women expressed intent to continue receiving advocacy services (Gondolf, et al., 1988).

African American women's ability to escape a violent relationship has been compromised by the effects of discrimination, economic hardship, and social inequity (Sullivan & Rumptz, 1994). Sullivan & Rumptz found that African American women were more likely to live below poverty level, to have more children living with them, to be the sole provider for their family, and were less likely to have a car. They noted that health issues, material goods (furniture, household goods and supplies), and financial issues were most likely to be listed as needed resources in the first ten weeks of a shelter stay. Furthermore, financial and social issues affected

African American women, as well as other women of color, more adversely than European American women (Sorenson, 1996). For example, African American shelter residents participating in focus groups complained that shelters did not provide food that acknowledged different cultural preferences or appropriate grooming aids for African American women.

The National Black Survey, which examined African American help seeking behaviors for mental and emotional distress (Jackson, Neighbors, & Gurin, 1986), is the most comprehensive study of help seeking in the African American community. Study findings indicate that services were sought as a result of a physician, family member, or friend's referral. In the absence of more specific data, it seems important to carefully examine the beliefs, attitudes, understandings and expectations of the African American community at large regarding help seeking, including assistance in cases of domestic violence. The authors of this study consider community attitudes toward help seeking in cases of domestic violence in the African American community through the use of focus groups.

Methods

The focus group is a qualitative research strategy that uses a semi-structured discussion format. The group facilitator begins the process and moves the discussion along with the aid of discussion questions. However, the specific content and order of content are driven by participants' responses (Stewart & Shamdasani, 1990). It is a technique used to explore understudied issues or topics.

Participants

Twenty-seven, mixed sex focus groups were conducted in an urban, Midwestern city from May 2000 through mid-November 2000. Groups ranged in size from 3 to 12 members. Participants were volunteers. Recruitment was via newspaper advertisement and posted announcements. Participants received a twenty-dollar stipend for their participation. Participants were not permitted to participate in more than one group. A total of 201 African Americans (134 females and 66 males, one participant did not provide information) participated in discussions.

A brief demographic questionnaire was administered prior to participation. Participants ranged in age from 18 to 74 years, with a mean age of 35.8 years (SD = 12.9 years). They reported an average of 14 years of education, with a range of 8 to 22 years; and reported income ranging from 0 to $150,000, with a mean of $19,322 and a median income level of $18,000.

Procedure

An African American female, psychologist with eight years of experience conducting focus groups with African Americans led the sessions. A counseling graduate student assisted. The discussion of domestic violence was conducted in the context of mental health in the African American community; therefore participants did not necessarily have personal experience with domestic violence. Focus groups were 1 1/2 hours long and examined the mental health and domestic violence service utilization in the African American community. Four probes focused on domestic violence:

Participant perceptions of attitudes toward domestic violence in their community.

Barriers to seeking assistance and services.

Perceptions of needed services,

Knowledge of existing services.

Discussions were lively and participants appeared to share their thoughts, knowledge and experiences candidly. Several participants discussed personal experiences with domestic violence. Other participants discussed DV experiences of friends and family members. In general, participants had encountered domestic violence and were aware of its prevalence.

All discussions were audiotaped. The audiotapes were transcribed and independently reviewed by the authors. Shortly after group discussions, an assistant completed detailed field notes based on the sessions and debriefing discussions. Based on review of the transcripts, field notes, and debriefing notes, impressions were consolidated into a list of themes and issues.

Key Findings

Lack Knowledge of

Long term consequences of DV experience (everything is fine once a woman leaves)

Services (their location and costs)

Warning signs that violence is escalating

Cultural Values and Beliefs That Inhibit Disclosure

African American women are strong (pride) - deny violence, vulnerability

African Americans are responsible for themselves and others around them; as African Americans we take care of ourselves - self-blame, self-sacrificing, embarrassed, ashamed if unable to control or endure situation

African American women are responsible for keeping family together - avoid leaving (Have to consider effect of leaving on the children. How can you stop him from seeing his children?)

African Americans "don't tell their business" - deny, or avoid disclosure

Religious views (God will take care of it; pray; The Lord will change him)

Community Attitudes That Inhibit Disclosure and Intervention

Definitions of abuse (pushing and shoving are not serious)

Distrust of institutions (concerns related to police response to AA women, legal system involvement, and agency attitudes)

Loyalty issues, family pressure that inhibit self-disclosure and action (How can I (you) have him arrested? How could you leave him?).

I did nothing wrong. Why should I leave?

Rely on family, friends, and church for resources and referrals

Financial Concerns

How can I (you) survive?)

Treatment Needs
Community based, self-help support groups and networks

Self -esteem building to assist in leaving

Support and advocacy services to assist with issues after leaving (housing, job training, children's psychological needs)

Treatment, designed specifically for AA men, without stereotypes

Cultural Sensitivity
Sense that advocates and shelter workers understand that violence is not more acceptable in the African American community

Advocates and shelter workers who are perceived as comfortable communicating with AA women in a respectful, non-paternalistic manner

Diversity among advocates and shelter workers

Awareness of expectations sometimes incongruent with safety and well being based on community attitudes and values

Awareness that AA women respond to shelter rules within the context of a history of a controlling oppressive relationship and an oppressive society.

Implications
There is a need for education on domestic violence. Issues related to definitions, warning signs, behavioral cycles, and resources are required. The media outlets and institutions

prominent in the African American community must be targeted. Because African Americans rely on family, friends, and the church for information and referral, outreach must be broad. Women will likely consult with one of these sources for support prior to action. Advocates must find ways to facilitate this social support system throughout a woman's effort to address her domestic violence experience.

Diversity and sensitivity require ongoing awareness and action. Shelters must systematically examine staff composition and training. Advocates and shelter workers must be knowledgeable of cultural values, community attitudes, and social experiences that may affect reactions and responses to domestic violence. This knowledge should be differentiated from myths and stereotypes related about domestic violence in the African American community. Communication strategies that facilitate positive and supportive interactions between advocates/workers and African American women, who have experienced DV, should be included in training modules. Shelter rules and policies should be examined to discern how they might impact diverse populations, and how explanations or implementation can be made more culturally sensitive.

Conclusion

Participants were aware of the need for services that addressed domestic violence in the African American community. Despite this recognition, lack of knowledge, cultural issues, and community attitudes were noted to impede action by abused women and support from friends and family. These barriers can and must be addressed.

References

Gondolf, F (1988). Battered women as survivors: An alternative to treating learned helplessness. MA: Lexington Books.

Hampton, R. L. and Gelles, R. J. (1994). Violence toward Black Women in a Nationally Representative sample of Black Families. Journal of Comparative Family Studies, 25, 105 _ 119.

Jackson, J. S., Neighbors, H. & Gurin, G. (1986). Findings from a National Survey of Black Mental Health: Implication for Practice and Training. In M.R. Miranda & H. L. Kitano (ed.). Mental Health Research and Practice in Minority Communities: Development of Culturally Sensitive Training Programs. Washington, D. C.: U.S. Government Printing Press.

National Violence Against Women Prevention Research Center (2001). Fostering collaborations to prevent violence against women: Integrating findings from practitioner and researcher focus groups. Charleston, SC: Author.

Rennison, C. (2001). Violent victimization and race, 1993-98. Bureau of Justice Statistics Special Report (NCJ Publications #, NCJ176354). Washington, D. C.: U. S. Department of Justice.

Stewart, D. W. & Shamdasani, P. N. (1990). Focus groups: Theory and practice. Newbury Park: Sage.

Sorenson, S. B. (1996). Violence against women: Examining ethnic differences and commonalties. Evaluation Review, 20, 123-145.

Sullivan, C. M. & Rumptz, M. H. (1994). Adjustment and needs of African American women who utilized a domestic violence shelter. Violence and Victims, 9, 275-286.

Thomas, E. K. (2000). Domestic Violence in African American and Asian American communities: A comparative analysis of two racial/ethnic minority cultures and implications for mental health service provision for women of color. Psychology: A Journal of Human Behavior, 37, 32-43.

U. S. Department of Justice (2001). Criminal Victimization Bureau of Justice Statistics

Feedback Join Us Site Map VAW Prevention Home

AmeAfrican American Attitudes toward Domestic Violence and DV Assistance

Vetta Sanders Thompson, Ph.D. & Anita Bazile, Ph.D.

Current data indicate that despite a more than two-decade decline, African American women continue to experience a higher rate of intimate partner homicide compared to women of other races. In addition, African American women's rates of intimate partner violence are higher than every other group's, except American Indian women (U.S. Department of Justice, 2001). Contrary to expectation, African American women are more likely to make reports of intimate violence to the police than women of other racial/ethnic groups (Rennison, 2001). National surveys of prevalence and a growing body of literature on domestic violence among African American women have highlighted the need for data on attitudes toward DV services, perceptions of treatment/intervention needs, and evaluation of DV programs in the African American community. Advocates and practitioners have voiced concern over the lack of research that addresses why African American women are less likely to access victim services (National Violence Against Women Prevention Research Center, 2001).

There are few studies examining the needs of African American women experiencing domestic violence. Studies suggest that African American women do use domestic violence services (Thomas, 2000; Sullivan & Rumptz, 1994; Gondolf, Fisher, McFerron, 1988). Gondolf, et al. (1988) noted that most women, regardless of race or ethnicity, sought the same amount but different kinds of help, such as financial support from social services agencies or family, shelter services, counseling from ministers, friends, or agencies; as well material items from friends, family, or agencies. This early study using Texas shelter data (N=5708) indicated that African American women were more likely to call a minister or the police. Sullivan & Rumptz, (1994) suggest that African American women may seek services at the point that violence becomes life threatening, with African American women reporting more severe abuse in the 6 months prior to entering a shelter than European American women.

African American women benefit from domestic violence services. For instance, Sullivan and Rumptz (1994) indicated that African American women who received advocacy services were more satisfied with their stay and had a higher quality of life at follow-up. These services included assistance with education and acquisition of household items. After services were received, African American women expressed intent to continue receiving advocacy services (Gondolf, et al., 1988).

African American women's ability to escape a violent relationship has been compromised by the effects of discrimination, economic hardship, and social inequity (Sullivan & Rumptz, 1994). Sullivan & Rumptz found that African American women were more likely to live below poverty level, to have more children living with them, to be the sole provider for their family, and were less likely to have a car. They noted that health issues, material goods (furniture, household goods and supplies), and financial issues were most likely to be listed as needed resources in the first ten weeks of a shelter stay. Furthermore, financial and social issues affected

African American women, as well as other women of color, more adversely than European American women (Sorenson, 1996). For example, African American shelter residents participating in focus groups complained that shelters did not provide food that acknowledged different cultural preferences or appropriate grooming aids for African American women.

The National Black Survey, which examined African American help seeking behaviors for mental and emotional distress (Jackson, Neighbors, & Gurin, 1986), is the most comprehensive study of help seeking in the African American community. Study findings indicate that services were sought as a result of a physician, family member, or friend's referral. In the absence of more specific data, it seems important to carefully examine the beliefs, attitudes, understandings and expectations of the African American community at large regarding help seeking, including assistance in cases of domestic violence. The authors of this study consider community attitudes toward help seeking in cases of domestic violence in the African American community through the use of focus groups.

Methods

The focus group is a qualitative research strategy that uses a semi-structured discussion format. The group facilitator begins the process and moves the discussion along with the aid of discussion questions. However, the specific content and order of content are driven by participants' responses (Stewart & Shamdasani, 1990). It is a technique used to explore understudied issues or topics.

Participants

Twenty-seven, mixed sex focus groups were conducted in an urban, Mid Western city from May 2000 through mid-November 2000. Groups ranged in size from 3 to 12 members. Participants were volunteers. Recruitment was via newspaper advertisement and posted announcements. Participants received a twenty-dollar stipend for their participation. Participants were not permitted to participate in more than one group. A total of 201 African Americans (134 females and 66 males, one participant did not provide information) participated in discussions.

A brief demographic questionnaire was administered prior to participation. Participants ranged in age from 18 to 74 years, with a mean age of 35.8 years (SD = 12.9 years). They reported an average of 14 years of education, with a range of 8 to 22 years; and reported income ranging from 0 to $150,000, with a mean of $19,322 and a median income level of $18,000.

Procedure

An African American female, psychologist with eight years of experience conducting focus groups with African Americans led the sessions. A counseling graduate student assisted. The discussion of domestic violence was conducted in the context of mental health in the African American community; therefore participants did not necessarily have personal experience with domestic violence. Focus groups were 1 1/2 hours long and examined the mental health and domestic violence service utilization in the African American community. Four probes focused on domestic violence:

Participant perceptions of attitudes toward domestic violence in their community.

Barriers to seeking assistance and services.

Perceptions of needed services,

Knowledge of existing services.

Discussions were lively and participants appeared to share their thoughts, knowledge and experiences candidly. Several participants discussed personal experiences with domestic violence. Other participants discussed DV experiences of friends and family members. In general, participants had encountered domestic violence and were aware of its prevalence.

All discussions were audiotaped. The audiotapes were transcribed and independently reviewed by the authors. Shortly after group discussions, an assistant completed detailed field notes based on the sessions and debriefing discussions. Based on review of the transcripts, field notes, and debriefing notes, impressions were consolidated into a list of themes and issues.

Key Findings

Lack Knowledge of

Long- term consequences of DV experience (everything is fine once a woman leaves)

Services (their location and costs)

Warning signs that violence is escalating

Cultural Values and Beliefs That Inhibit Disclosure

African American women are strong (pride) - deny violence, vulnerability

African Americans are responsible for themselves and others around them; as African ricans we take care of ourselves - self-blame, self-sacrificing, embarrassed, ashamed if unable to control or endure situation

African American women are responsible for keeping family together - avoid leaving (Have to consider effect of leaving on the children. How can you stop him from seeing his children?)

African Americans "don't tell their business" - deny, or avoid disclosure

Religious views (God will take care of it; pray; The Lord will change him)

Community Attitudes That Inhibit Disclosure and Intervention

Definitions of abuse (pushing and shoving are not serious)

Distrust of institutions (concerns related to police response to AA women, legal system involvement, and agency attitudes)

Loyalty issues, family pressure that inhibit self-disclosure and action (How can I (you) have him arrested? How could you leave him?).

I did nothing wrong. Why should I leave?

Rely on family, friends, and church for resources and referrals

Financial Concerns

How can I (you) survive?)

Treatment Needs

Community based, self-help support groups and networks

Self -esteem building to assist in leaving

Support and advocacy services to assist with issues after leaving (housing, job training, children's psychological needs)

Treatment, designed specifically for AA men, without stereotypes

Cultural Sensitivity

Sense that advocates and shelter workers understand that violence is not more acceptable in the African American community

Advocates and shelter workers who are perceived as comfortable communicating with AA women in a respectful, non-paternalistic manner

Diversity among advocates and shelter workers

Awareness of expectations sometimes incongruent with safety and well being based on community attitudes and values

Awareness that AA women respond to shelter rules within the context of a history of a controlling oppressive relationship and an oppressive society.

Implications

There is a need for education on domestic violence. Issues related to definitions, warning signs, behavioral cycles, and resources are required. The media outlets and institutions prominent in the African American community must be targeted. Because African Americans rely on family, friends, and the church for information and referral, outreach must be broad. Women will likely consult with one of these sources for support prior to action. Advocates must find ways to facilitate this social support system throughout a woman's effort to address her domestic violence experience.

Diversity and sensitivity require ongoing awareness and action. Shelters must systematically examine staff composition and training. Advocates and shelter workers must be knowledgeable of cultural values, community attitudes, and social experiences that may affect reactions and responses to domestic violence. This knowledge should be differentiated from myths and stereotypes related about domestic violence in the African American community. Communication strategies that facilitate positive and supportive interactions between advocates/workers and African American women, who have experienced DV, should be included in training modules. Shelter rules and policies should be examined to discern how they might impact diverse populations, and how explanations or implementation can be made more culturally sensitive.

Conclusion

Participants were aware of the need for services that addressed domestic violence in the African American community. Despite this recognition, lack of knowledge, cultural issues, and community attitudes wer'e noted to impede action by abused women and support from friends and family. These barriers can and must be addressed.

References

Gondolf, F (1988). Battered women as survivors: An alternative to treating learned helplessness. MA: Lexington Books.

Hampton, R. L. and Gelles, R. J. (1994). Violence toward Black Women in a Nationally Representative sample of Black Families. Journal of Comparative Family Studies, 25, 105 _ 119.

Jackson, J. S., Neighbors, H. & Gurin, G. (1986). Findings from a National Survey of Black Mental Health: Implication for Practice and Training. In M.R. Miranda & H. L. Kitano (ed.). Mental Health Research and Practice in Minority Communities: Development of Culturally Sensitive Training Programs. Washington, D. C.: U.S. Government Printing Press.

National Violence Against Women Prevention Research Center (2001). Fostering collaborations to prevent violence against women: Integrating findings from practitioner and researcher focus groups. Charleston, SC: Author.

Rennison, C. (2001). Violent victimization and race, 1993-98. Bureau of Justice Statistics Special Report (NCJ Publications #, NCJ176354). Washington, D. C.: U. S. Department of Justice.

Stewart, D. W. & Shamdasani, P. N. (1990). Focus groups: Theory and practice. Newbury Park: Sage.

Sorenson, S. B. (1996). Violence against women: Examining ethnic differences and commonalties. Evaluation Review, 20, 123-145.

Sullivan, C. M. & Rumptz, M. H. (1994). Adjustment and needs of African American women who utilized a domestic violence shelter. Violence and Victims, 9, 275-286.

Thomas, E. K. (2000). Domestic Violence in African American and Asian American communities: A comparative analysis of two racial/ethnic minority cultures and implications for mental health service provision for women of color. Psychology: A Journal of Human Behavior, 37, 32-43.

U. S. Department of Justice (2001). Criminal Victimization Bureau of Justice Statistics

Feedback Join Us Site Map VAW Prevention Home
National Violence Against Women Prevention Research Center © Copyright 2000
(843) 792-2945/telephone (843) 792-3388/fax

Footnotes. reference notes;

HTTP://EN.wikipedia.org/wiki/michelle_obama

www.squidoo.com/michelle-obama

http://en.wikipedia.org/oprah winfrey

www.womenshealth.gov   minority/african   american/
obesity.cfm

www.feminist.com

www.brandeis.edu

http://en.wikipedia.org dorothy_heights

www.soulwork.net

www.lectlaw.com/files/fam27.htm

Web Du Bois "Africana Encyclopedia" footnotes
By. Editors Kwame Anthony Appiah, Henry Louis Gates
Jr. Harvard University
Basic Civitas Books 1999
Assata Shakur pg.1697
Shirley Chisolm pg.424
Fannie Lou Hamer pg.915
Mary McCloud Bethune pg.229
Sara Walker pg.1697
Nefertiti pg.1403
Myrlie Evers pg. 1515
Corretta Scott King pg.1324
Cleopatra pg. 464
Betty Shabazz pg.1679
Angela Davis pg.564
Michelle Obama pg. 103
Maya Angelo pg. 103